Can you survive?

T0328007

Contents

Written by Claire Llewellyn

Collins

brown bear

rattlesnake

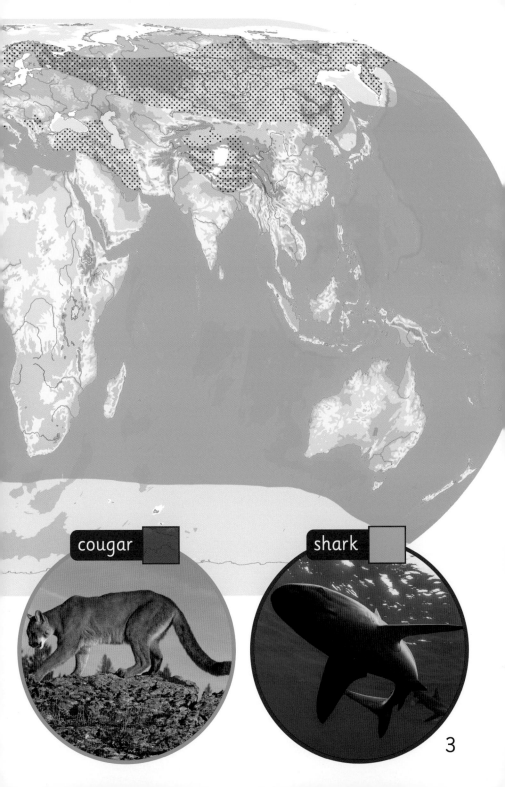

cougar

shark

3

Picture the scene ...

You're walking along a forest path when you meet a bear. Would you freeze? Or run away?

We all enjoy exploring nature, but it can be dangerous. Learn the right and wrong things to do when you meet a wild animal.

5

Beware of snakes!

Most snakes are harmless but a handful are **venomous**. You should always be prepared.

- Wear trousers and sturdy footwear.
- Never lift rocks with bare hands.
- Listen for rustles in dry leaves.

What should you do if you meet a snake?

- Stay calm and slowly back away.

- If the snake bites you and **punctures** the skin, wash it with water.

- Fetch a doctor – fast!

rattlesnake

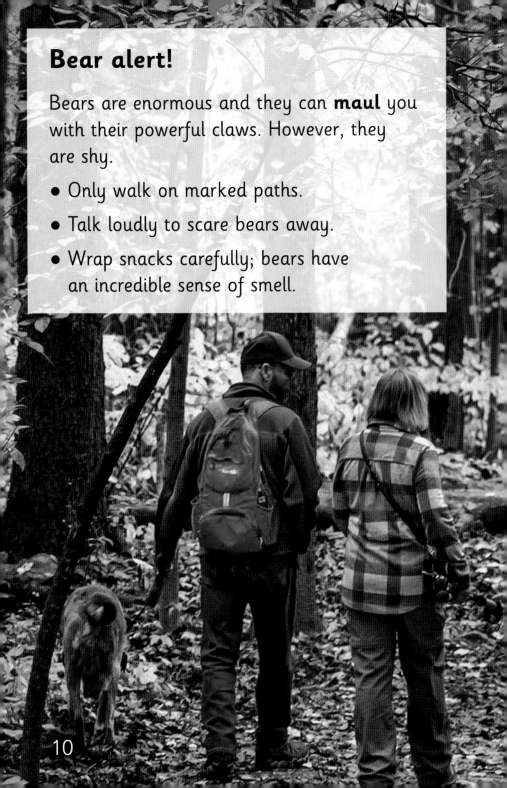

Bear alert!

Bears are enormous and they can **maul** you with their powerful claws. However, they are shy.

- Only walk on marked paths.
- Talk loudly to scare bears away.
- Wrap snacks carefully; bears have an incredible sense of smell.

10

What should you do if you meet a bear?

- Freeze! Don't run away.
  Back away slowly instead.

- Never stare at the bear.
  Bears might see it as **aggressive**.

- Don't pause to take a photo.

Shark alert!

Most sharks never come near humans and shark attacks on humans are rare.

- Don't swim where sharks live in the early morning or after dark. That's when they hunt.

- Swim in groups. Sharks are less likely to attack groups of people.

- Don't wear a wristwatch that glistens in the water. Shiny things could look like fish **scales**.

What to do if you meet a shark in the water

- Get out of the water as fast as possible.
- Don't splash, it might attract the shark.
- Alert any people nearby.

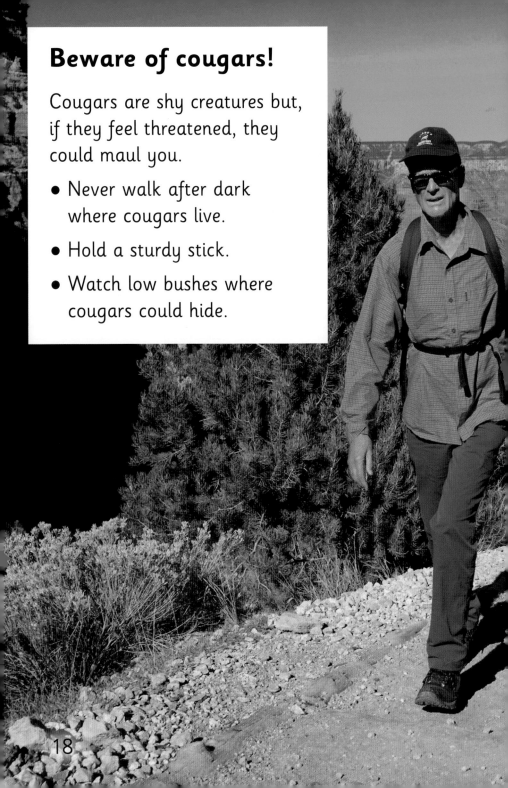

Beware of cougars!

Cougars are shy creatures but, if they feel threatened, they could maul you.

- Never walk after dark where cougars live.
- Hold a sturdy stick.
- Watch low bushes where cougars could hide.

What to do if you meet a cougar

- Freeze and stare at the cougar.
- Raise both arms to appear taller.
- Walk back slowly.

So now you are prepared! But remember, if you are able to visit a place where these animals live, take care! Respect nature, be careful and do not venture out without a well-prepared adult!

Who is better prepared?

Glossary

aggressive threatening and ready to attack

maul to attack by scratching and tearing

punctures makes a hole with something sharp

scales the shiny covering of a fish

venomous when an animal's bite or sting
  contains poison

Close encounter with a shark

There have been some near misses with sharks.

This shark swam directly under surfers who didn't notice it until it was almost too late!

A teenager captured it all on his drone from the air and called the emergency services.

Close encounter with a bear

A boy was hiking with his mother in the US. They spotted a bear sunning itself in the woods. The boy's mother quietly told her son to sit down. The bear glanced over and saw they weren't a threat and went back to sunning itself.

Can you survive?

What would you do if you met these animals?

🐾 Review: After reading 🐾

Use your assessment from hearing the children read to choose any GPCs, words or tricky words that need additional practice.

Read 1: Decoding

- Focus on reading words with /air/ and /ur/ sounds. Ask: Which letters make the /air/ or /ur/ sound?

  wear (/*air*/ *ear*)   **beware** (/*air*/ *are*)   **where** (/*air*/ *ere*)

  learn (/*ur*/ *ear*)   **doctor** (/*ur*/ *or*)

- Challenge the children to read the page headings in bold fluently. Say: Can you blend in your head when you read these headings?
- Bonus content: Challenge the children to read page 28 fluently, sounding words silently in their heads.

Read 2: Prosody

- Model reading pages 4 and 5 to the children as if you are presenting a survival documentary.
- Ask the children to work in pairs to prepare their own reading of these pages. Ask: What tone will you use? Which important or interesting words will you emphasise?
- Encourage children to take turns to read a page to the class.

Read 3: Comprehension

- Ask the children: What wild animals do you think are the most dangerous – why? What would you do if you saw one?
- Ask: What is the book telling its readers? (e.g. *how to survive dangerous animals; how to prepare for the wild*) Discuss other possible titles for the book based on this. (e.g. *Survival! Prepare for the wild!*)
- On page 4, point to the word **freeze**. Ask:
  o Does this mean "turn to ice" or does it mean something else in this context? (e.g. *it means immediately keep still/stop moving*)
  o What makes you think this? (e.g. *it's about people, who can't turn to ice; it's compared with "**run away**"*)
- Give the children the following statements and ask: Is this true or false? Why?
  o Bears' paws are gentle. (*false: they can maul*)
  o The golden rule is: Always run away! (*false: e.g. you freeze if you see a bear or a cougar*)
- Turn to pages 30 and 31. Challenge the children to sum up how to be prepared for each animal.